ANCIENT KEMITE ISLAM

and the

PRESERVATION OF MA'AT

THE MISSING LINK BETWEEN ANCIENT AND MODERN CIVILIZATION

Written by: Cozmo Ali El, The Minister of Culture

The Preface

The Chief Karim-Bey Speaks

We greet our beloved brothers and sisters in the greetings of peace, and from the sacred olive groves of Kemet to the halls of learning in America.

Our subject topic today is Kemet (Egypt). Many scholars attribute Kemet to being the homeland of civilization.

It is true that much of the so called modern world has taken the example if the Kemite (Egyptian) structure for civilization.

Let us take a brief look at this Kemite phenomenon.

As far back as the Western world can trace themselves and their institutions is back to Akhenaton of ALKEBU-LAN known as Kemet.

The order and structure of this present day society is the exact same as it was in Kemet, only in opposite relationship the white supremacy vs. black supremacy etc.

The various conceptions of reality that make up the elements which are defined as Egyptian or Modern Roman-American (European political economic and social structures) were and are contained within the Kemet ic model of Masonic Tradition.

A closer observation of such documented accusations can be found in the book "STOLEN LEGACY," written by George G.M. James.

The USURPATION of the head of Universal Government, as dethroned within the centers of learning in effect maladjusted the cultural nationalistic tendencies in the aboriginal social structures. Which in turn educated or separated the people from their original source of reference or reality? One of the main fallacies is to get people to believe the origin of civilization was not and is not a product of Islamism (Scientific working principles of Ma'at i.e...Living Ma'at).

Many sly devils will have you believe Al-Islam is a product of civilization. All these concepts are incorrect and these so called scholars have no power to produce the effects that the scientists of Al-Islam produced. Namely the Nabi-Muhammad Ibn Abdullah (p).

However, there are some that are able to recognize in the light of regeneration in the Mauritania with its unfoldment in the Moorish invasion of Europe. Yet and still these scholars fail to give clarity and exactness in their science due to fear of being dethroned and thus coerced to follow the same path of Egypt, and the Moorish Empire of yesterday. In attempting to usurp the sovereignty of the Creator of the universe.

THE REVOLUTION CONTINUES!

Chief Karim-Bey

INTRODUCTION:

Inheritors of Kemite (ANCIENT MOABITE) culture.

It was the ancient Kemites who gave rise to so-called white civilization and this is well known among the Afro-centrics of today. It is also a matter of fact that these same so-called whites are largely responsible for the demise of ancient Kemite/Moabite civilization.

The seeming death of the Moabite way of life sent the western world (The part of the World under rule of the West) once illuminated by the great suns plunging into a realm of darkness, shame and superstition.

George G.M. James provides us with two figures of the conspiracy.

"As mentioned elsewhere, the Egyptian (Kemite) mysteries and the philosophical schools of Greece were closed by the edicts of Theodosius in the 4th century A.D. And Justinian in the 6th century A.D. i.e., 529, and as a consequence, intellectual darkness spread over the Christian Europe and the Greco-Roman world for ten centuries, during which time knowledge had disappeared." 1

Yes, disappeared only to reappear in a complete and preserved form for modern time. Chief Karim-Bey teaches us that this perfected form we speak of is none other than Islamic Moorish civilization.

Many Afro-Centric hold harsh feeling towards Islam. They deem it to be another mind control effort on the part of the western world under the guise of "religion."

They believe that the Arabs (whom they classify as white) enslaved the inhabitants of Africa not unlike the so-called white Christians enslaved our forefathers centuries ago.

However there are various flaws in these perceptions.

1. Was the Arab's culture so-called white?

2. Was Islamic civilization foreign to the inhabitants of Africa, the descendants of the Ancient Ones?

3. Were these so-called white Arabs really responsible for the light given

to the world by Islam?

4. What was the psychological effect of Islam as opposed to Christianity?

The answer to the question #1 has already been answered in this book.

The Arabs are descendants of Ishmael whose mother and father (Hagar and Abraham) were of Moabite blood, yet it was a Moabite tribe by the name of Jurham who taught Ishmael the language of Arabic.

Today, the main unifying characteristic among Arabs is the Arabic language, a South Semitic language from the Afroasiatic language family **Afroasiatic (Afro-Asiatic)**, also known as **Afrasian** and traditionally **Hamito-Cush**

Picture of a modern day Hadramaut Arab

"These original Arabs came from the Southern tip of the Arabian peninsula from what now is Hadramaut or Yemen." **2**

This book will show that the very language and culture of the modern day Arab is merely a reflection of the Ancient Kemetic way responsible for its birth. This book will clearly show the resemblance between Islam, the complete, and the Ancient Kemetic way of life.

However, in this introduction I will attempt to "kill three birds with one stone," i.e., Questions two three and four.

In order to do this let us refer to one of the pioneers of Egyptology brother George G.M. James.

"In the 8th century A.D. the Moors i.e. natives of Mauritania in North Africa, invaded Spain and took with them, the Egyptian culture they preserved." **3**

In The Alhambra - Rudolf Ernst (1854-1932)

Picture of a Moorish Moslem

We are taught the Moors he is referring to were mostly Moslem with some Moorish Jews. The principle invasion of Spain which marked the light of knowledge being born into the savage world, ending the dark ages was led by a Moslem General, Tarik. [See Gebel Al Tarik (Rock of Gibraltar)].

"As such the people of North Africa were the neighbors of the Egyptians, and became the custodians of Egyptian culture, which they spread through considerable portions of Africa, Asia Minor, and Europe. During the occupation of Spain, the Moors displayed the considerable credit, the grandeur of African culture and civilization." 4

"Had not the Moorish nation preserved the Kemetic (Ancient- Egyptian) sciences of geometry and astronomy, there would have been no way of calculating the months, seasons and years. Also without their contributions, global geography would not be as we know it today." 5

He also informs us that Moorish civilization was not limited to the borders of North Africa and Spain; rather he paints pictures of a vast kingdom directly linked to that of Ancient Moabites civilization.

They are fathers of civilization who inhabited this hemisphere since Antiquity." 5

Now let us turn our attention to question number four; the psychological effects of Islam as opposed to Christianity. Here I'll take the opportunity to refer to another pioneer of the now termed "Afro-centric conception Bro. Edward Wilmont Blyden. We are taught Mr. Blyden was one of, if not the chief influence upon Marcus M. Garvey. I will not take time here to expose his credentials, However, it would behoove one to undertake a study of his life and life's work.

His observation of Christianity:

"Owing to the physical, mental, and social pressures under which the African received these influences of Christianity, their development was necessarily partial and one-sided, cramped and abnormal. All tendencies to independent individuality were repressed and destroyed...All avenues to intellectual improvement were closed against them, and they were doomed to perpetual ignorance.." **6**

His comment is regards to Islam:

No sooner was he converted than he was taught to read and the importance of knowledge was impressed upon him." **7**

"Knowledge is power." How can one even begin to compare the two systems? The former of which gauged out the eyes and severed the tongues of those whose only crime was desiring to read or desiring to speak their native tongue, while the latter was a ladder to the pinnacle of wisdom and a light for even modern times.

Last, but not least, there is the question of the sword and it being a motivating factor in Islamic conversion. The Holy Qur'an clearly states,

"There is no compulsion in religion, the right direction stand forth, clear from error." **8** However, we know there are always those 'Devils' who say with their tongues what is not in their hearts. One cannot judge a code of life (Deen) by such people, as Deen is principles and principles themselves cannot be corrupted, though men may commit many an atrocity in their name.

Nevertheless, in the immortal words of Mr. Blyden:

"If the Mohammadean (Muslim) Negro had at any time to choose between the Koran and the sword, when he chose the former, he was allowed the latter as the equal of any other Muslim; but no amount of allegiance to the gospel relieved the Christian Negro from what he received with it, or rescue him from the political and - in a measure - ecclesiastical proscription which he still undergoes in all the countries of his exile. **9**

Islam is healthy and it is ours. It was the Moors (African Muslims) who gave the light of Kemet (Egypt) to the world again by way of the Moabite language of Arabic and Islamic Ritual. Hence a proper study of Islam as a revival and completion to the Moabite/Kemetic way of life is in order today.

May Allah guide this effort.

Cozmo ALI-EL

ONE GOD:

୩

_ |___Is the expression for God in the Ma'at u NTR (Holy Script) of the ancient Moabites (Kemites).

The phonetic value of ୩ is NTR.

A semblance can be made between the ୩ or NTR of the ancient

|

Moabites and the Moorish, Arabic symbol ا (Alif).

Arabic is the Holy Script of the Moors. Alif is also a symbol of God in the completion of Ma'at, <u>final Islam</u>, to who belongs the name of Al-Ahad (The

الله

Only). It is the first visual characteristic in the expression (Allah). It has the numerical value of Wahid or One.

The Ancient Kemitcs were essentially monotheistic in nature. There has been much discrepancy as to the use of the term god in the translating of Kemetic literature and Holy text. We are taught and it should be noted here that this term (god) equates to forces(s) of The God of the One God of Kemet. One God of Kemet was known as Ua NTR.

"The Egyptians called the creator of the universe Ua i.e...One or Ua Ntr is also called only one with a second." **10**

This reads very similar to a verse of the Holy Qur'an entitled "Sura tu Ikhlas," The Unity. It is also known as "Sura tul Ahad," The Only, Unique. It is the 112th Sura (chapter) and it states:

Say: He Allah is One, on He whom all depends, He begets not nor is he begotten and there is none like him."

Many become confused in regards to the God of the ancient Kemites. It would appear that He is given various names throughout the diverse Holy Scripts. There are also numerous symbols attributed to him due to the changes in terminology brought about by ever-evolving understanding of their spiritual orders.

Aten-Sun Force (RA)

Let us take the Aten of RA for example. It is said to be the sun. Are we to believe that the ancient Kemites with their high level sciences were so ignorant as to believe the actual physical sun was God?

"The One is of course Ra the sun god (Force) and the moon is Osiris. (Akhenaton) amen-Hetep IV says in his hymn to his god Aten i.e...solar disk, the physical body of the sun-God." "Thou art one alone [but there were millions of life in thee] God, one, there is no other [possessing] his power and attributes." **11**

Notice in the above quote the change in the term god to God. The sun-god is the force of light whereas God one (Ua NTR) is defined by Amen-Hetep V as a unique being by which all things subsist. God was expressed in various ways, among them Ra, Aten, Temm etc...

"But whether the God address be called Ta-tenen, or RA, or Amen RA it is always the Sun-God (force) or his home is the sun which is the mind of his worshiper." **12**

In the complete Islam there is a sign not unlike the sun and it also holds deep significance to the Muslim (submitter). It is known as the Kaba.

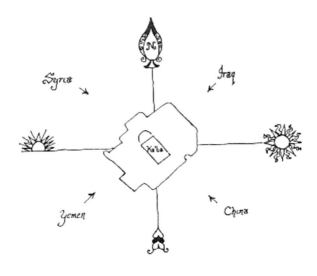

In fact, the term Kaba is composed of words and concepts from the ancient Moabite concept of the soul.

Spiritual Body		Sense
Akh		
Ka		
Ba		
Khat		
Ren		
Khaibit		
Ab		

"The Ka was a term that referred to the creature and preserving powers of life...the Ba represented the soul or the spiritual side of man." **13**

The KABA represents the sun, as pilgrims journey to the Holy City of Mecca annually in order to rotate seven times around what is termed the House of God (Bait ul Lah). This is can be said to be symbolic of the Earth's yearly rotation around the sun.

According to science there are seven days in a year viz. Sunday, Monday, Tuesday, Wednesday, Thursday, Friday, and Saturday. In the Arabic language these days are known as Yowmi Ahad (Day one) Yowmi Ithnayn (Day two) Yown tha Latha (Day three) etc... There are no other days we know of; they simply repeat themselves over and over suggesting a circle or rotation.

Though the KABA is known as the House of God (Allah.) It is purely symbolic. The Muslims are aware He, God, cannot be house within a cube.

The KABA is symbolic of man or mind. KA - you, Ba - mind, which is according to the Holy Qur'an enlivened with the breath of Allah's spirit

(Divine ideas or Noor.)

"Behold thy Lord said to the angels; I am about to created man, from sounding clay, from mud molded into shape: when I have fashioned him (in due proportion) and breathe into him of my spirit fall down in prostration."**14**

But what is the Sun?

What meaning does it hold that men of all ages should be in such awe about it?

The sun is a great source of light and life for our universe. It is 93,000,000 miles away from our planet. Its diameter is 853,000 miles. The rays of the sun causes the Earth to travel around it in what is termed the "earth's orbit." It gives life to solar system by providing us with heat and energy.

All plant life reach up towards its unceasing glow. It draws the water up into the atmosphere in a mist causing clouds to form. Once the water is heavy enough, it falls back to the earth resurrecting the dead earth-life.

It is because of this, the sun has become a symbol of great force. However, the ancient Kemties were not mere pagan worshipers. The Sun was a sign or symbol of light and life which must manifest through the minds and hearts of the believers. The Kemites must have known as we do today that though the Sun provided all the above, it was not God, The One , The Only.

It has already been mentioned in an earlier chapter that the Sun represents the mind of the worshiper or the home of knowledge and light of God supreme. This concept is prevalent in the Holy Qur'an as light of God (Noor) illuminating the mind (home of the believer.)

"Allah is the light of the heavens and the earth. The parable of light is like a niche and within it a lamp: the lamp enclosed in a glass: The glass as it were a brilliant star: lit from a blessed (olive) tree neither of the east nor of the west, whose oil is well-nigh luminous, though fire scarce touch it: light upon light! God doth guide whom he will to his light: God doth set forth parables for men: and God doth know all things." **15**

From this Sura we can clearly see that God is not a literal light. We can also see it is not the intention of God that we should worship light or Sun - <u>the brilliant star</u> and through the superstitious among men are afraid of such parable or analogies He, God is not.

Now where doth this light reside? This we are told in the next verse.

"In the home, which Allah hath permitted to be raised to honor. For celebration in them of his name. In them he is glorified morning and evening (again and again)." **16**

SALAT AND THE SUN

Another interesting point that must be considered is the salat (ritual prayer) which itself is observed according to the position of the sun in the "Heavens." Here are some examples;

FARJ: There are five ritual prayers of the final Islam, the preservation/ completion of Ma'at. The first of which is performed directly before sun rise, hence the name Salat ul Sabh (The Morning Prayer). It is also known as Salat ul Farj. The word farj has its origins in the Arabic root F R J meaning to separate for split. In this case farj must refer to the Sun's appearance separating night from day.

THOHR: the second ritual prayer is known as Thohr (Midday Prayer) and is offered immediately after the Sun has reached its meridian.

The word thohr comes from the Arabic root TH H R which means to become perceptible, clear, manifest come into light, overcome, conquer, etc.

We get the definition conquer and overcome from the Sun's apparent ascension or climb to the peak. This is symbolic of conquering ones lower self. It is interesting to note that at this point there is practically no shadow or shade.

This word Thohr bears much resemblance to the Greek (mediator) Thor. Thor was said to be the "mediator between heaven and earth or the higher mind and the lower natures in the soul." **17** However, Thor is the Greek version of the ancient Kemite Thoth.

THOTH   SYMBOL FOR HERMES OR
GREEK VERSION OF THOTH

THURSDAY – after Thor, Teutonic god of war

THOR'S HAMMER

(PEGAN SYMBOL)

Thoth is said to be the husband of Ma'at (Harmonious order, submission). Thoth is divine intelligence and clear word which is the expression of perfect perception. He represented the faculty of reason or in other words clarity of mind.

The sun is also quite important in the complete Islam as a purifier of things that become impure. In the book if Islamic Jurisprudence of Ayatollah Khomeni (R.A.H.) it states "Earth, buildings, windows, and other immovable objects which are difficult to be ritually purified with water becomes ritually pure once the ritual impurity is removed, by the sun shining on them..." **18**

With these examples it will suffice to say, the Sun as a symbol of light, clarity of mind, and life is one of high station to the adherents of the final and complete version of Islam (Harmonious submission) as it was to the ancient Kemites.

THE COMPLETION OF MA'AT (ISLAM)

My use of the phrase preservation/completion of Ma'at might prove confusing for the reader; hence an explanation is in order. We can see and Chief Karim-Bey co clearly explains in the preface, that owing to the superstition of most of those religious, the masses have been put under the illusion that Al-Islam is a new phenomenon. This conception is not sustained in the Qur'an nor the history of mankind.

The founder (Prophet) of Islam was not the first Prophet to teach Ma'at (order or orderly submission) rather he was the seal of the Prophets (khatimu Nabi).

The Holy Qur'an is not the first revealed book, but it was the final revolutionary book of God, Thus term completion Ma'at.

"Nothing is said to thee that was not said to the apostles before thee; that their Lord has as His command all forgiveness as well as a most grievous penalty." **19**

According to the Qur'an the message was the same, and this same message is from the same one and only God.

"And question thou our apostles whom we sent before thee, did we appoint any deities other than (God) Most Gracious to be worshiped? **20**

Upon reading the verse one cannot help but to call to mind the ancient Moabite Amun known for his grace and patience.

"The priest of Amen were never tired of proclaiming the greatness and majesty of Amen...the Egyptians generally held

Other views about him and that they are ascribed to him the character of a compassionate and gracious God, who was long suffering and of great goodness." **21**

The term Amun means the Hidden One. In the Completion of Ma'at (Islam), Allah has many attributes. One being Al-Batin or The Hidden. It is believed by the mystics that if this name is recited "three times each day one will be able perceive the truth in things." **22**

ABRAHM (SUN OF HAM)

AMEN HOTEP AND SOLAR DISK ATEN

There is a likeness in the history of Akhenaton, (Amen -Hetep IV) and that the history of the Prophet Ibrahim (Abraham). Akhenaton tried to replace the material form of god as sun (Aten) with that of Amen and as a result became a great threat to the established religious order of his day.

"Another indication that Abraham had the necessary knowledge to enter Egypt (Kemet) is the fact that he learned by looking at the stars, moon, and sun." **33**

Abraham observed the stars, moon, and sun in sequential order. Through somber reflection he was able to perceive the truth of the matter. More powerful and awesome was the creator of such illustrious and illuminating signs.

He was most impressed with the sun until he was penetrated by divine Noor (light).

"When he saw the sun rising in splendor he said: that is my lord; this is the greatest but when it is set, He said; Oh my people; I am now free from your guilt of ascribing associates to Allah. For me, I have firmly and truly fixed my face towards him who created the heaven and the earth and never shall I give partners to Allah." **24**

This account in the Qur'an clearly shows a relationship in the stories of these two great prophets.

There are those who slander the Prophet of the Completion of Ma'at (Islam), calling the unlettered prophet a plagiarist. I ask these so-called Afro-centric can truth plagiarize itself? The Qur'an bears testimony to the fact that Islam is not a new way of life, instead it is a completion and perfection of the ancient way (Milla).

One might say even that ancient Kemites gave birth to Islam. Islamic history records this event. Ibrahim (Abraham) was indeed a Moabite and in the beginning held much the same view as the materialist concept of God, yet he came to the same conclusion taught in the mystery schools of Kemet through his God-given talent of reflection.

Hagar, the wife of (Ibrahim) Abraham was also of Kemetic blood.

"Abraham was married to Sarah for several years before he married Hagar who was from Egypt (Kemit)." **25**

Now Hagar was the mother of Ishmael and it is through this line that the Prophet Mohammad (p) came forth.

Ibrahim was not unlike Mohammad (p) for he (Ibrahim) represents a single stage of purification of the completion of Islam.

THE SUNSET AND THE HORIZON

Al-Qur'an states that when the Abrahim saw the sunset, He came to the resolution that the sun was a sign (ayat) of the creator or The One God (Ua NTR).

The term sunset has its origin in Kemet. Set represented the sky's force of the night, the usherer in of darkness, this the sunset. His celestial counterpart was Hor, Her, or Horus, from which we derive the term horizon. Hor was the sky force of the day (rays of the sun's light).

Set therefore came to personify darkness and evil of the material world. He represented all kinds of wickedness. In a sense, he symbolizes the setan, i.e., satan or shayton.

We are taught the term shayton from which we derive the English satan is a combination of the ancient Kemetic terms, Set and Typhon, thus saton or Shayton.

"Initially in the Golden Ages, Typhon and Nephthys were beneficent, but as time went on, as heaven and Earth began to separate, they and Typhon in particular came to be malevolent, bent upon chaos and destruction." **26**

In other words, then the Earth (impulse, nature, or material) was dis-joined from Heaven (the Higher- self, Allah's ideas in man). Typhon then became bent on malice and destruction. Shayton did not become or manifest his devilishment until man was brought into being he was confronted with the test of submission. Prior to this event, he was known as Iblis the Gin, which is a free will creature like Man with the exception that Gins are created from fire whereas Man was made principally from water, breath (air) and clay. Although, there is no element we (Man) do not consist of. Shayton's rebelliousness led him to be cast out of Heaven along with his followers.

"And behold, we said to the angels bow down to Adam: and they bowed down but Iblis, he refused and was of the (arrogant) disbelievers." **27**

"And the Gin race was created from fire and scorching wind. **28**

Shayton was taken over with vanity, pride, and arrogance and as a result he was cast out thereafter he also became malevolent directing his negativity at Mankind. He promised to be and we are warned in the Holy Qur'an that he is "an open enemy."

"Set like the One God had many names and had captains and servants and followers which were known as the sons of Set (Setsons) the Mesu betesh the children of rebellion." **29**

In the Moorish/ Arabic language <u>Masay</u> is evening or around time of the sunset and <u>betesh</u> is a tyrannical oppressive and ruthless person.

Set was the opposite and equal power of Horus and those forces strove against each other. The sun rose every morning and the sunset every evening and therefore one never overcame the other. the impossibility of one overtaking the other is mentioned in the Holy Qur'an.

"It is not permitted that the sun catch-up to the moon, nor can't he night outstrip the day; each float along in an orbit." **31**

HORUS

The Prophet (Nabi) Mohammad (p) is like Hours. That is not to say the Prophet could not overpower Shayton (Set). History (hadith) record the Prophet "had no shadow," as the sunlight of the horizon has not shadow. In order for an object to had a shadow, it must be and an obstacle for light rays. Since sunlight is the source of illumination for our solar system, it does not exist in such a way as to block itself. It cannot therefore have a shadow.

The Prophet (p) had no shadow (lower-self), because he absorbed the divine light (Noor) and he thus became a transmitter of the light of Allah.

He is like Horus in the sense that Shayton (Set) is an open adversary to prophets and mankind until the day when he is sentenced to hell.

"Verily Shayton is an enemy to you: so treat him as an enemy. He only invites his adherents, that they must be his companion of the blazing fire." **32**

Hence the two light and darkness shall exist in this world until we as believers absorb the Noor as did the Prophet.

"The day you shall see the believing men and women how their lights run ahead of them and by their right hands (greeting) Good news for you this day! Gardens beneath which rivers flow, to dwell therein for aye, this indeed is the high triumph." 33

"Light runs ahead of them" this could possibly be a result of absorbing the Noor and thus is what is described as running ahead is a transmission of light.

Thus, the Prophet (perfect man) can be lightened unto the day light force Horus of the ancient Moabites.

SALAT FOUND IN KEMET (Egyptian Hieroglyphics)

The Egyptian God Horus

If it is true that the ancient language and or script lead to understanding the minds of ancient cultures, then let us briefly view some Maat u NTR characteristics:

Character #1 is a man standing upright with his arms extended forward bent at the elbows, palms almost directly in front of his face. The phonetic value of this character's tua, means to pray, to entreat, to adore. In this position, the adherent of Islam offers hi intention to perform the prescribed number of Rakats (cycles) of the ritual prayer (salat).

This position is also known as Qunut in the salat of the Shia or Ahlu Bait, the pure teachings of the house of the prophet.

Character #2 phonetic value is also tua like the Muslim'sdua. thisformofsupplicationcanbefoundintheHajj ritual of the Muslim today.

"The performer of tawaf (7 circuits around the KABA) should stand towards that corner of the KABA where the black stone in embedded in its walls in such a means as to have it ones right and give utterance to the niyyat of performing tawaf in these words:

"Oh Allah, I intend to perform the tawaf of the consented premises, make accept it from me. Then facing the Black stone and raising the hands with the palms outwards, one should say: "I begin in the name of Allah and all praise is due to Allah, and Allah is the most Great and peace and blessings be on Allah's apostle." [34]

Character #3 bears much resemblance to the position in salat was well. It is a picture of a man bowing. This meaning is to bow or pay homage to.

the Muslim bows and pays homage to UA NTR (On God) in the position of ruku. It is in this opposition the Muslim says: Glory be to my Lord the Mighty one or three times.

Character #4 is a man standing upright with is arms hanging down by his sides. this position symbolizes submission.

also exists in the Muslim salat. It is known as Qiyam (standing position). It is in rule that the present day Muslim rises to Qiyam. saying:

"Allah has listened to him who praised him, glory be to my Lord with His praise.

In fact this is the position in which salat begins.

In the many characters of Maat u NTR we find another picture word that resembles the modern Muslim salat. It is a picture of a man kneeling on his knees while sitting back on his feet. Its meaning is that of a dead or holy being. It is my belief that death here does not refer to physical death but implies one has died to his lowerself.

Character #5 is the exact same position of the salat known as jalsa (sitting). Rising from ruku, then prostrating, then sitting back on the knees, one performs what is termed Jalsa. In this position, one testifies to the oneness of God and the apostleship of Mohammad (P.B.U.H.A.H.P.).

More information can easily be attained by a review of the determinative signs of Maat u NTR or for that matter the whole of Maat u NTR script. It is astonishing however to this author that many expert Afrocentrics appear to overlook such obvious relationships between the Moabites and the final way for humanity, the completion (Islam) or is it that there is a conspiracy to X Islam out of the Afrocentric picture? This Question I leave to the reader to answer.

LINGUISTICS

Amongst the obvious relationships between the ancient Moabite way of life and the completion of Ma'at is language. This chapter is a brief comparative study of Holy Scripts, Hymns, Poetry, etc. of the ancient Moabite and their inheritors (Moslems).

Arabic - hsb:

to count, calculate, make equal

Maat - hsb:

to count

Arabic - Khaber:

intelligence, bringing forth of news of information

Maat - Khepru:

the sun force called Khepri in the morning at sunrise, as it brought forth the light or good news ending physical and mental darkness

Note: letters B and P are phonetically interchangeable.

Arabic-Ray	to see, perceive, or conceive of an idea, which is oftentimes symbolized especially in cartoons) as a light bulb shining in one's head
Maat-Ra	sunforce of the ancient Moabites, in other words, Noor (divine light).
Arabic-Seth or Sethy	to level of plane, the outer, external, or superficial
Maat-Set	the sun's force setting which appears to be level in the western sky. It is was the worldly and external

Arabic-NuNu	Arabic colloquial for baby which is brought forth from a liquid despised (semen)
Matt-NuNu	Ancient Moabite force which ruled liquid mass. Abyss of slime he was a hermaphrodite which may refer to the period in which the sex of the child in the womb is undetermined.
Arabic-Haras/ Haris	Superintendent, overseer, watcher, guardian
Maat-Horus	Day light sky force of heavenly power, whose symbol is the falcon. Ie. overseer.
Arabic-ASR	The point in which the sun is between high noon and sunset. Descending toward night only to appear in the east again at Farj (morning).
M a a t - A s i r , Osir, Osr	The ancient Moabite forcer which became ruler of the after world, was also resurrected by his wife, Isis
Arabic-Asiy or Asa	To nurse, treat a wound, also to grieve, to be distressed.
Maat-Isis	Wife of Asir and Mother of Horus. Treater of Heru when he was attacked by venomous snakes, magical healing power, she became distressed and frantic while searching for her dead husband, resurrector of Osir.
Arabic-Maat or Maata	to seek to establish a link to extend, to enter into relations, related by matrimonial link, als ones kinship, family ties.

	a reciprocal relations hip between forces, harmonious submission of the created o the law and order.
Maat-Maat	

Maat is performing ones natural and divine obligations, by way of a ritual (prayer, fasting, good action, etc...). This in turn unite heaven (man) and earth (woman) or in other words, it establishes the harmonious relationship between humanity activity.

Maat then is Islam (peaceful submission) for the benefit of micro- as well as macro-societies. the ethical ties which created harmony between human forces giving purpose to our earthly existence.

Adam prayed for Maat which is recorded as him praying for a Kaba or a balance between Ka and Ba which he and his descendants could circulate or use as an axis like the one he saw in the heavens the bair ul mamur.

The Kaka was rebuild by Abraham and Ishmael and Ma'at was perfected by Allah through His messenger, Mohammad.

ANCIENT MOABITE SCRIPTS AND QUR'AN (BRIEF COMPARATIVE STUDY)

ON SUCCESS

INSTRUCTINS OF AMENEMOPE

CHAPTER 1

If you spend a little time with these things in your heart, you will find it good fortune: you will discover my words to be a treasure house of life, and your body will flourish on earth.

HOLY QUR'AN

CHAPTER 24,51

The answer of the believers when summoned to Allah and his Messenger, in order that we may judge between them is no other than "we hear and obey." It is such as these that will prosper. It is such as obey Allah and his Messenger and fear Allah and do right, that will triumph.

ON GOOD SPEECH

AMENNMOPE

CHAPTER 1

Do not get into a quarrel with the argumentative man nor incite him with words; Proceed cautiously before and opponent and give way to adversity; sleep on it before speaking, for storm comes forth like fire in hay is the hot-headed man in his appointed time.

HOLY QUR'AN

CHAPTER 17, 53-54

Say to my servants that they should only say those things that are best; for satan doth sow among them: for satan is to man an enemy. You Lord knoweth best: If he please, he granteth you mercy, or if he please punishment.

ON WORLDY GAIN

AMENNMOPE

CHAPTER 7,9, 10

DO not set your heart upon riches, for there is no one who can ignore destiny and fortune. Do not set your thought on external matters: forever man there is his appointed time. Do not exert yourself to seek out excess and your wealth will prosper for you.

HOLY QUR'AN

CHAPTER 28, 60

The material things which yea are given are but conveniences of this life and the glitter thereof, but that which is with Allah is better and more enduring; will ye not then be wise?

ON DEPENDENTS

AMENNMOPE

CHAPTER 11

Do not covet the property of a dependent, nor hunger for his bread; but the property of the dependent blocks the throat. It is vomit for the gullet (Perhaps limited property of the poor). If he has engaged in false oaths his heart slips back inside him...

HOLY QUR'AN

CHAPTER 4:2

To orphan restore their property (when they reach age) or substitute (your) worthless things for their good ones; and devour not their substance (by mixing it up) with your own. For this is indeed a great sin.

ON MAN

AMENNMOPE

CHAPTER 25

Man is clay and straw and God is his potter. He is overthrown and he builds daily.

HOLY QUR'AN

CHAPTER 95:4

We have indeed created man in the best of molds.

CHAPTER 6:2

He it is who created you from clay...

THE HYMN TO THE ATEN

VERSE 6

You have placed seed in woman and have made sperm into man who feeds the son in the womb of his mother, who quiets him with something to his crying.

HOLY QUR'AN

CHAPTER 22:5

Oh mankind! If ye have a doubt about the resurrecting (consider) we have created you out then out of sperm, then out of clot, then out of morsel of flesh, partially then out a clot, then out of a morsel of flesh partially formed and partly unformed, in order that we may manifest (our power) to you and we cause you to rest in the wombs for an appointed term...

I think not!

How can this be?

It is simple. Messengers came in every time and clime and with the same message from the same one God who is a symbol of light i.e. Noor or Re for his creatures

FOOTNOTES

1.   Stolen Legacy, George G.M. James pg. 30

2.   Introduction of Al Ajrumia Sankore Institute

3.   Stolen legacy pg. 39

4.   Ibid

5.   The Fallen Moorish Empire, Dhanifu Sayyid Karim-Bey

6.   Islam, Christianity, and the Negro Race

7.   bid

8.   Sure Tu Bakara Ayat 256

9.   Islam, Christianity, and the Negro Race

10.   Ancient Egyptian Theology, E.A. Wallace Budge pg. 6

11.   Ibid

12.   Ibid

13.   Abraham's Legacy, Mustafa El Amin pg. 61

14.   Sura 15, verse 28-29

15.   Sura 24,verse 35

16.   Ibid verse 36

17.   Dictionary of Scripture and Myth. G.S. Gaskell

18.   Islamic Jurisprudence pg. 57 part C

19.   Sura 41:43

20.   Sura 42

21.   Ancient Egyptian Theology, E.A. Wallace Budge

22.   Ninety Nine Names of Allah pg. 95

23.   Abraham's Legacy, Mustafa El Amin pg. 32

24.   Sura 6:78-79

25.   Sura 6:38

26.   Abraham's Legacy pg. 41

27.   The Egyptian Mysteries

28.   Sura 2:34

29.   Sura 15:27

30.   Ancient Egyptian Theology pg. 8

31.   Sura 36:40

32.   Sura 35:6

33.   Sura 57:12

34.   Elementary Teachings of Islam pg. 76, 77

PART II

TABLE OF CONTENTS

Through Love and Purity Only The Divine Thought Pattern Will

Understand

INTRODUCTION

Before consuming the knowledge in this book, one should know that there are some classical differences, in the cultured Moorish perception of Kemite (Ancient Egyptian) portents and stories and that of Greco-Roman (European) interpretations.

It stands to reason that since the ancient Moabites (Kemites i.e., Hamites) came to use picture words, letters, etc. as a form of communication as well as visual expression, the written word for God would possess an image.

However the written expression for God was not intended to be the physical form of God, no more than the written expression ALLAH (The Supreme Deity in the cultured Moorish Language of Arabic).

To those who would refute this, let us propose a question: What is ideograph?

Answer:

1. Just as Maat u Ntr (Hieroglyphics) represent the actual picture so do

they represent ideas. For example, take "   a hall in which deliberations by wise men were made represents the idea of counsel. " **1**

Also the   which is symbolic of God, One or (Ua Ntr). This symbol is also likened unto an "AXE." 2. It is used, in metaphorical terms, by the godly to cut away the useless part of character.

2. In the cultured Moorish Language of Arabic though the picture word is no longer in use, the word itself often holds an idea.

Take the very word Islam, the word Islam most commonly means peaceful submission. When one hears the word with a common understanding he naturally thinks of the Middle East and the religion founded 1,400 years ago by Mohammad Abdullah (servant of god). However the ideas carried in the body of the term Islam reaches to the far ends of the Universe because Allah (The Supreme Deity) is Rabi Al Ameen, Lord of the Worlds. **3**

Islam is a real concept of creation, order, and a way of life. It is as much a way of life for the birds and the bees as it is for Human Beings, because we are told in the Qur'an "seek they other than Allah's Religion (Deen)? And to Him submits, whoever is in the heavens and the earth, willingly or unwillingly, and unto Him they will be returned." **4**

In order to embark on the journey to harmony with oneself, surroundings, and the Creator, one   must set out on the SIRAH (Path). i.e., Sirat Al Mustaqeem (the upright Path, the Path, Maat,   "Right and Truth")**5**. Hence the idea behind the written word Sirah as opposed to its general meaning.

This tradition of preserving, if you will, the esoteric meaning of things is an ancient Moabite science which is demonstrated in the Moorish Way (Deen). In fact, the ancient / Arabic, Abjad (Alphabet) was initially arranged in a manner to deliver inner meaning.

"The original letters were as follows:

A, B, J, D, H, W, Z, H, T, Y, K, L, M, N, S, AI, F, S, Q, R, SH, T, TH, KH, DH, D, and GH." **6**

As opposed to the modern:

A, B, T, TH, J, H, KH, D, DH, R, Z, S, SH, S, D, T, TH, AI, GH, F, Q, K, L, M, N, H, W, Y, L-A, H.

"In ancient times the Arabic (Arabic speakers) said: Abjad hawwas huttiya kalimanna sa'afsa qarashat thakhadha daddhaghalla. Which meant: Adam refused obedience and became impassioned with the eating of the tree and slipped and fell from heaven to earth. His error degraded him; he ate from the tree and he was favored with repentance. He rebelled and was taken out of blessings, then he admitted his sin and was saved from punishment.7

Thus, written expression is a conduit for precious knowledge which at its highest level of development should hold both obvious definition and inner esoteric meaning.

The term god and sense perception in general

Regarding the miscalculation and false assumptions of the Greco-Roman concerning Divinity, it should be noted here that throughout this book the term god and sometimes God will be accompanied by the word force in parenthesis like so (force).

The reason for this being, there is only one Supreme Deity (Ua, Ntr, Allah), the term God itself is derived, we are taught, from the Moorish / Arabic word Yad (hand) however from an allegorical stand point it represents the ability to act or exert force.

We are told in the Holy Qur'an on the day of Judgment hands and feet shall speak and expose the liars [see the Holy Qur'an, resurrection].

In other words hands and feet (actions and deeds) would expose the truth of one's life sum, hands are the vehicle by which we "do" or "exert our force."

It is our intention to arrive at truth minus confusion and error; hence let us endeavor to scrutinize sense perception in general and its insufficiencies.

Genealogy of the Supreme Deity

A man* inquired of Abu Jafar: Inform me about the Deity since when had he been in existence? The Imam replied: When did Allah not exist? so that I may tell you since when He has been in existence. Glorified is he who has been in existence eternally and who will exist eternally. The Unique, The Eternal, Absolute. Never has he taken Himself a consort or a son.

There are two types of men. They are man-made men and there are God-made men. The man-made mind is finite and limited. Man himself is an eternal being. The very simple proof of this is his eternal abode. Man as a non-eternal being would have no use of an everlasting abode or state if in fact his existence was of a finite nature. Be it a heavenly or a Hellish state, this eternal abode we are promised in the Qur'an as well as the bible and various other scriptures.

Man-made man is thus termed finite because of his mental growth and development. There is a natural process of the production of mind as well as an artificial one. All artificially produced minds are limited to the programming of their designers. This is much like the capability of a computer. The computer or computer program cannot function outside of its design and is because of this restricted in its capabilities. Like this, so is the artificially produced man in his conception of himself, life, the Supreme Being, etc...hence the question of our finite inquisitor as to the beginning of Allah.

The beauty of the response is a perfect example of God-made mind. What could be a more perplexing question than "when did your Lord begin?" The question itself pre-supposes the beginning of Allah and thus laying the burden of proof on the Questioner. Nevertheless the (Imam) remarks "when did he not exist?"

Man was placed in the earth at a certain stage of its development. He would not exist in the earth before the earth was cooled because the molten conditions of the planet would render it impossible for him to survive physically. Thus physically, not ideally, earth land existed before physical man, creation is laid out for us when we arrive on this plane hence the Creator of the heavens and the earth must have existed before these as well.

How impossible would it be then for one to know the beginning of the Creator since man as physical creation was not present to witness even the creation of the heaven and earth.

Now one might say: Human beings were not in attendance during many creations, yet due to science and investigation we may now possess information regarding intricate details of many things. This information includes the birth of beings that physically out date us.

It is for this purpose the Imam proclaims the uniqueness of Allah and disassociates from Him the reproductive process i.e. consort and son.

*Muhammad ibn yahyaibn Muhammad-Al Hasan ibn Mahmud-Abi Hamza as saying Nafi ibn Al Azraq ibn Qays Al Hanifi, Abu Rashad [d.65/685] the head of Azariqah – one of the great sects of the Kharajites

All things in our Universe are considered capable of being investigated through the six senses.

1. Touch

2. Taste

3. Smell

4. Hearing

5. Sight

6. Intellect

Allah cannot be comprehended in Knowledge because all these faculties are rendered ineffective when endeavoring to perceive Allah. However, there are those who believe that if the Supreme Being cannot be attained by the eye or comprehend knowledge, He is not real and should therefore be denied.

"Abu Abdullah stated: Oh son of Adam, if a bird were to feed upon your heart it would not be satisfied with hunger. and if the eye of a needle were to be put over your eye the whole of your eye (vision) would be covered. With such (insignificant) instruments i.e. the heart and the eye, indicating the thinking and the senses, do you really intend to comprehend Allah's vast dominion of the heavens and the earth? And if your claim (to understand) Allah is rightly valid, there here is the sun which is a (very small) creation from among Allah's creations. If you can meet it with your two eyes, you are right in your claim."

It is commonsense that if one were to stare directly into the sun his look would return to him confused and injured, so it is when one sets out to peer into the essence of Allah's secret knowledge. One whose goal is to perceive the Supreme Deity in His Entity injures himself.

To summarize it in poetic terms:

1.   Had He been visible we would have studied him.

2.   Had He been tasteable, we would have devoured him.

3.   Had He been audibly hearable, we would have drowned out His sound.

4.   Had He been perceivable through the smell, bad odors would have replaced his scent.

5.   Had He been touchable, we would have defiled him.

6.   Had He been Understandable by intellect, we would have solved all His mysteries.

7.   Thus is Our Lord Above all attributed to Him.

MAY ALLAH GUIDE THIS EFFORT

CHAPTER ONE

Heliopolis-Mecca in Kemit (Egypt)

Heliopolis now reduced to a small suburb in Cairo, was once the focal point of trade, commerce, and religious order in Kemet. Heliopolis or City of the Sun, was in pre-dynastic times the most important city in Kemet.

"it was in terminus of many caravan routes from East, North-East, and South-East, and the starting point of caravans going to Libya and Nubia, and countries further South, and its temples waxed rich through the offerings and merchants and travelers. It was a great central market...beside all it importance as a religious center was so great that the priesthood influenced, if not actually controlled the religious beliefs of the Egyptians down to the close of the dynastic period." **1**

If the above quote is beginning to sound familiar, it must be due to the reader's knowledge of Mecca in Saudi Arabia, the Cultured Moorish Holy city.

As mentioned in part II of this series (Resolution of the Age part II), Chief Karim –Bey teaches us that the KABA represent universal order. This is why the pilgrims travel annually to circulate it (KABA) seven times. The rotation of the KABA in the twelfth month of Hajj is symbolic of the earth's complete orbit around the sun. Seven is symbolic of a complete cycle as in seven days in a week. There are 52 weeks in a year, 5+2=7, thus seven circuits around the KABA. However the sun is not the only commonality of these two great cities.

Numbers as Ideographs

The Holy City of Mecca prior to the advent of the Prophet was also one of economic enterprise. It too was controlled by Religious Order. Not unlike the priesthood of Heliopolis, this religious order's power was principally due to wealth and influence, and the idols (false gods) were their true economy.

It is reported that three-hundred and sixty idols were destroyed by the

Prophet Mohammad p.b.u.h.a.h.p. upon recapture of the KABA from the hands of the materialist.

Interestingly enough, it seems that the structure of the theological system in Heliopolis resembles that of pre-Islamic Mecca.

9x3=27=2+7=9

360=3+6+0=9

Three-hundred and sixty idols would virtually be one idol for every day of the year making their (Mecca) system complete. Nine in esoteric terms is complete as in the nine months of human gestation. In fact, the "priest of Heliopolis suffixed the name to Ra." **2**

It would seem the word temm has made its way into the Moorish language of Arabic meaning "to become complete."3

The Black Stone of Kemit

Heliopolis-city of the Sun bears much in common with the Holy City of Mecca than one might be aware of, therefore let us proceed further into this great city.

"The principle temple of the sun was in Heliopolis...housed in a sacred stone, the ben ben." 4

This mini mound, a pyramid shaped stone was believed to be the first piece of Earth created.

The Holy City of Mecca also housed a sacred stone Al Hujra tul Aswad; The Black Stone. It was held to be the first remains from which Adam (first complete man) was created by Allah i.e. Ua Ntr, the One God from black mud, clay

Zam Zam of Heliopolis

"There was a well at Heliopolis which was most holy, for tradition said that the Sun-God (Sun-Force) bathe his face in its waters when he rose on this earth for the first time." 5 There is also a Holy well in Mecca. This well is connected with miraculous event of Islam; its name is Zam Zam.

"...this well quenched the thirst if Hagar (a Moabite woman) and her son Ishmael, when mother and child were abandoned in this barren furnace valley before there was Mecca...Mohammad the child, Mohammad the man, Mohammad the Prophet p.b.u.h.a.h.p. drank of these sacred waters. It was his habit to drink from the well of Zam Zam at the close of his **tawaf** (rotation of the KABA)." 6

The well of Zam Zam was discovered by Hajar, wife of Ibrahim/ Abraham while deserted in the scorching desert by Ibrahim upon Allah's command.

Water the Source of All Life

One does not have to be reminded of the importance of the Nile in ancient Kemetic life, whether it be social, economic benefits or the theological significance surrounding it. Nevertheless, "...the first piece of ground which was created was held to at Heliopolis, still more important was the belief that the Nile of the North rose at Heliopolis."7 This place was known as the "House on the Nile."8

Now let us reflect on the significance of the water soured which gave birth to Mecca. After a frantic search which is re-orchestrated by pilgrims during Hajj rituals, she notice the well water seeping out of the ground. "When overcome by anxiety, Hajar looked towards the place where she had put down her child, she beheld that water was gushing from the earth, and flowing in all directions...seeing the precious liquid escaping into the sand, she cried, 'zumi mubarak' that is 'come together oh waters of the Divine Providence" and a pool formed."9

Later a Moabite tribe by the name of Jurham settled, by Ibrahim's leave, thus the population of Mecca was born. After which, Ibrahim and his son Ishmael built the KABA in this valley in which it had previously stood.

To summarize it in simple terms,

a.   Water is the source of all life:

      1.   The social economic, spiritual, and even the physical existence of the Holy City of Mecca has its roots with the emergence of a mystical well or water source, the Zam Zam as does all life.

      2.   Keep in mind this Holy City not only contains the House of Allah for worship but it also connected with the Black Stone (like ben ben) and thus connecting it with the history of the first man, Adam. Adam himself is related to Atum or Aten or Heliopolis (See Atum chapter 2).

Chapter Two

Atum-Adam of Heliopolis

ATUM, first of all, was "always depicted as a man."**10** He was represented as Pharaoh (Ruler) and his very name suggests that he was complete.

ADAM was the first man to be completed with the breath of Allah's Spirit. He was place in the earth to be a Khalif (Ruler).**11** "So when I have made him complete and breathed into him of My Spirit, fall down making obeisance to him."**12** Atum begot future generations just as Adam is attributed to being the father of us all, the Human family. He (Atum) thus represents the creative god (force) by which Ua Ntr (One God) used to produce life or populate the planet.

"Atum joins himself to Ptah and acts as a Demiurge and executes the work of creation." **13** Ptah is symbolic of the Mind, Divine Thought or Divine Word.

In order to fully understand Atum, one must undertake discussion of Ptah.

PTAH means the opener as the Kemite word for to open is ptah, pronounce taw. Interestingly enough, Ptah can be said to be related to the Cultured Moorish phatah, pronounced F-taw which means opening (of a way to victory). This word is derived from the Arabic root PH-T-H, meaning to open. The word phatiha is also derived from this same root, it is the opening sura (chapter) in the Holy Qur'an of Mecca.

It comprises of seven verses.* it is the foundation of the Muslim salah (ritual prayer) and it is recited on the norm ten times per day, minimum. Phatiha has been termed the "Ummul Qur'an" the essence of the whole Qur'an: **14** The seven verses of the Phatiha form the foundation of the psychology of the reciter and polishes his outlook of God-Allah, Self, and the Universe.

Ptah of Kemet is the divine creative word and is also known as the "Divine Potter." **15** Remember Allah says in the Qur'an that He fashioned or molded Adam (first man)**16** Likewise, and we have already stated earlier that Adam was created from black mud clay. Allah also says: when he intended to create a thing he merely says "kun fa ya kun;" "be, and it is".

Hence Ptah is the higher ideas and principles of truth and light (Noor) by which Allah i.e. Ua Ntr molds man, which is mind.

If one was to know his Egyptology, own world know that "Ptah is the first to rise from the primeval waters of (Nun) earth in the form of a hill, closely following the hill the God (creative force). Atom also emerges from the waters and sits on Ptah (the hill)." **18**

Thus Atum was elevated by Ptah (mind principles) where he derives the powers to created and govern as Khalif i.e., Pharaoh or in other words Ruler.

Regarding the description of Adam's creation, Ali ibn Abu Talib says, "Allah collected form hard, soft, sweet, sour earth clay which He dipped in water until it became pure and kneaded it with moisture until it became gluey...then He (Allah) blew into it out of His Spirit whereupon it took the pattern of a human being with mind that governs him, intelligence which he makes use of, limbs that serve him." **19**

But Atum was also associated with the sun for he "represented the evening or night sun."**20** Can we find any such similarity in the creation of Adam, which according to Ali is made principally from earth clay, moisture/ water, and air (Breath of Allah)? The answer is yes.

After Adam was completed with the Breath of Allah's Spirit, Allah commanded the angels and heavenly beings to submit to Adam. "Be prostrate towards Adam and they prostrated, except Iblis." **21**

*1. In the name of Allah, the Beneficent, the Merciful. 2. All praise is due to Allah, Lord of the worlds.

3. The Beneficent, the Merciful. 4. Master of the day of Judgment. 5. Thee alone do we worship, Thee alone do we seek for aid. 6. Show us the straight path, the path of those whom you have bestowed grace. 7. Not the path of those whose portion is wrath nor those who go astray.

Iblis was created from fire and pride withheld him from submission "so that he took pride in his creation of fire and treated contemptuously the creation of clay (Adam)."22

It should be noted here that Iblis or Shayton, the equivalent of the Kemite Set, prior to the manifestation of Adam was of high rank over the Angels. However, since his Adam's appearance, he (Adam) has not been able to disunite himself from the presence of the Gin of fire, Iblis.

As a result of disobedience, Iblis was cursed, "...for verily thou art driven away accursed.." 23

He was however respited his punishment until the last day (judgment). "Then you are of the respited ones." 24 There after, Allah placed Adam in the paradise. In other words, elevated him in rank among the godly. "Then his enemy Iblis envied his abiding in paradise and his contacts with the virtuous...he thus converted his happiness into fear and his prestige into shame." 25

Adam then learned some words from his Lord which brought him back to Allah's favor. "And Allah turned to him mercifully..."26 After which according to Ali, He (Allah) "...sent him down to the place of trial and procreation." 27

Summary

Atum – rose out of the water of the earth (Nun)

Adam – was made from clay and dipped in water and kneaded with moisture

Atum – was elevated on Ptah (the hill)

Adam – was elevated to paradise

Atum – was depicted most often in the form of a man, Pharaoh (Ruler)

Adam – was the first man and khalif (Ruler)

Atum – symbolized completeness

Adam – was completed by the Breath of Allah's Spirit

Atum – was known as the creator of men

Adam – begat the human family.

Atum – merged with Ptah (Divine word) and executed creation

 Adam – received revelation (Divine words) and was favored, he executed the creation of Divine mind or thought pattern.

Atum – was associated with the night sun

Adam – was associated with Iblis, the Gin of fire, also as recipient of revelation (Prophet) he would certainly symbolize Divine light in mental darkness

Spiritual Numerology (Living Math i.e. Maat)

There are in fact numerous relationships in that of the Cultured Moorish and Kemite conceptions and theological systems. Among them we find what we shall term Spiritual Numerology.

Many so-called conscious African American minds might be familiar with, as a result of the teachings of the Honorable Elijah Muhammad (science of Living Mat-a-Matics). See next page.

However, this knowledge extends from much further back in history than the N.O.I.* movement, "we also understand that the Egyptian attached numerical value to both letters of words and geometrical figures, with the same intention as with their use of hieroglyphics, in oder to conceal their teachings." 28

In other words to place or rather derive an idea within a common source of reference for the purpose of educating those seeking higher learning.

This tradition of preserving the higher theological idea within a baser form was performed by both the ancient as well as the modern Arabic [Arabic is the only language of the Cultured Moors (Clock of Destiny)].

Science of Living Mathematics – Moorish Color Code of Electronics

1. KNOWLEDGE

2. WISDOM

3. UNDERSTANDING

4. CULTURE

5. POWER

6. EQUALITY

7. god or yad (creative Force)

also perfection

8.   BUILD AND DESTROY

9.   BORN

10. CIPHER – everything must pass through the cipher.

0 –Black hole

1- Brown

2 – Red

3 – Orange

4 – Yellow

5 – Green

6 – Blue

7 – Violet

8 – Grey

9 – Light or White

Clock of Destiny C.M. Bey

Our Moorish Forefathers harnessed atomic energy …centuries before the red-skinned blondes. Patagonia had become educated by cultured Moors.

Ancient Alphabet (Abajdiyyah)

abjad

hawaza

hutiya

kalamna

sa'afsa

qarashat

dhazaghum

1 = Adam (at) one with Allah's commands

0 = Spiritual

0 = Mental

0 = Physical

The Three trimesters

This arrangement teaches about the Fall of man (Adam) see introduction pg 3. It begins with the numbers 1, 2, 3, 4, and ends with 1, 0, 0, 0. Now 4 is symbolic, in this case, of the earthly or carnal mind state as abjad symbolized Adams refusal and disobedience. 1, 0, 0 , 0 can possibly refer to his conquering of self and earthly nature by admission of his sin and was saved from dazaghum.

The Curriculum of the Priesthood

Many, due to insufficiency of knowledge, believe that Muslim priests (Imam) are only learned in matters of religion, however this is a fallacy. There is extensive study that precedes one recognition as an Islamic Moorish leader.

Upon entering this road of training the first level or grade is Mujtahid (one who endeavors to practice juristic reasoning). In Kemet we find "a priest was also a judge and interpreter of the law."**29**

The mujtahid is defined as one who practices ijtihad (seeking to struggle), from which we derive the word jihad (definite struggle) of which there are two types:

1.   Jihad i Asghar

2.   Jihad i Akbar

Jihad i Akbar is the minor or external struggle, whereas the Jihad i Akbar is the Major struggle i.e. the struggle against lower self.

In Kemit we find "Neophytes were graded according to their moral efficiency and intellectual competence, and had to submit to many years of tests and ordeals, in order that their eligibility for advancement might be determined. Their education consisted of the Seven Liberal Arts and Virtues. The virtues were not mere abstractions or ethical sentiments but positive valorous and virility of the soul. Beyond these the priests entered upon a course of specialization. 30

There are also courses of specialization within the Islamic Moorish curriculum, however due to time and space we shall undertake that study more extensively at another duration.

Now let us compare the prerequisite training of the Neophyte with the Mujtahid, shall we?

Neophyte – Seven Liberal Arts

1. Grammar

2. Arithmetic

3. Rhetoric

4. Dialect i.e. the Quadrivurn

5. Geometry

6. Astronomy

7. Music (G.G.M. James – Stolen Legacy)

Mujtahid – Education

1. Arabic Grammar (to the extent required)

2. Exercises in deduction so that the power of the deduction develops

3. Knowledge of colloquialisms

4. Language of the Qur'an and sunnah (traditions of the Prophet)[Islamic Jurisprudence pg 34].

5. Geometry falls under specialization training such as the knowledge needed in building a masjid (mosque).

6. The word Moor means to navigate as we were master Astrologers and ruler of the Seven Seas.

7. Music was replaced by Melodic Qur'anic recital.

There are many more extensive studies or grades and levels in both the Kemite and the Cultured Moorish schools. Nevertheless, we believe the information in this chapter will suffice as proof (hujjah); the relationship between the former and the latter.

Conclusion

Through LOVE and PURITY only the Divine thought pattern will understand. Due to the abundance of information in Part I and II of this series, Resolution of the Age, we shall keep our final comment brief, for the Knowledge speaks for itself. Thus let there be no more talk about some Arab religion called Islam. Instead, let us recognize this complete and perfected way of life as the final code of standards given to the world by Allah, Ua Ntr or whatever name you choose, through our ancient forefathers and completed by His Prophets.

Footnotes:

1. Egyptian Language E.A. Wallace Budge pg . 28

2. Circle Seven Koran-ology

3. Chapter 2 of the Holy Qur'an

4. Ibid

5. Right and Truth is one of the definition of Maat, see Book of the Dead (Negative Confessions)

6. Sankore Institute (Al-Ajrumiay)

7. Ibid

----

2. Ibid

3. Hans wehr Arabic Dictionary

4. The British Museum Book of Ancient Egypt pg. 60

5. A.E. Theology pg.13

6. A Guide to Hajj S.A. Husein pg. 71

7. A Guide to Hajj S.A. Hussein pg. 71

8. Ancient Egyptian Theology, Wallace Budge pg. 1

10. Egyptian Book of The Dead, Wallace Budge pg. cxi

11. Sura (Chapter) 2:30

12. Ibid

13. George G.M. James, Stolen Legacy pg. 140

14. A Guide to Hajj S.A. Hussein pg. 71
15. Ancient Egyptian Theology, Wallace Budge pg. 13

16. History of Hajj

17. Egyptian Book of The Dead, Wallace Budge pg.

cxi

18. Sura (Chapter) 2:30

19. IBID

20. George G.M. James, Stolen Legacy pg. 140

21. Sura 2:34

22. Nahjul Balagah pg. 93

23. Sura 15:34

24. Sura 15:37

25. Nahjul Balagah pg. 9

26. Sura 15:3

27. Nahjul Balagah pg. 76

*Nation of Islam

28 Stolen Legacy pg.133

29 Stolen Legacy pg. 32

30Ibid

Made in the USA
Middletown, DE
29 June 2021